The 7 Habits of Highly Objective People

The 7 Habits of Highly Objective People

David Kelley, Ph.D.

The Atlas Society Press

Published by
The Atlas Society Press
800 Rockmead Drive, Suite 200
Kingwood TX 77339

Library of Congress Cataloging-in-Publication Data:
Kelley, David, 1949–
The 7 Habits of Highly Objective People / David Kelley
ISBN 978-1-7326037-7-6

Printed in the United States of America

Cover design by Matthew Holdridge
Book layout by Andrei Volkov

Contents

Introduction

What do the following situations have in common?

- Tyler is a libertarian in a political argument with someone who advocates raising the minimum wage. As the exchange progresses he becomes increasingly impatient and begins hurling at his opponent every objection that comes to mind.
- Dr. Weiss is seeing a patient whose symptoms mostly fit the syndrome for depression, despite some anomalies. In a hurry to see the next patient, he ignores the anomalies and prescribes an antidepressant.
- Carla's husband has started coming home late from work, and seems more distant when he is home. She can't bear to think he's having an affair (which he is), so she convinces herself he's working harder to support the family.

What these individuals have in common is a lapse of objectivity. Tyler is invested in proving he's right about the issue; he is using debating points instead of stepping back to consider what's essential to the issue; he is not trying to understand the opponent's case. Dr. Weiss is ignoring the anomalous symptoms that weigh against his diagnosis. Carla is making up a story to evade a suspicion that scares her.

Objectivity is a core element of rationality, a cardinal virtue in the Objectivist ethics—and in any moral code that aims to help people live their best lives. As a mental orientation and practice, objectivity has two essential elements. 1) It means, first of all, a commitment to finding the *truth*. It means recognizing that **reality is what it is**, independent of what we think or feel about it. Facts are facts. 2) But facts do not reveal themselves to us automatically. Knowledge of reality has to be acquired by a complex process of thought that is self-directed and subject to error. So the second element of objectivity is the commitment to using the *methods* of reason, a cognitive capacity that has a specific nature, operates in a specific way, and is subject to specific constraints.

Objectivity is therefore both a virtue and a skill—a virtue because it is a chosen commitment to truth and reason, a skill because the methods of thinking have to be learned. We learn the methods of objective thinking in the course of education, training, and experience over the course of our lives. Like other skills, these methods become automated, like riding a bike. But never fully. We always have the choice to exercise these skills in the effort to grasp reality—or to evade, take short-cuts, or let emotions cloud our judgment.

When we say that someone is being objective, we mean that he is focused on reality, he is using logic to draw conclusions, he is trying to take account of all the relevant evidence, and he's willing to change his mind if new evidence supports a different conclusion. By contrast, a person is being subjective if his thinking is governed by bias or prejudice, if he ignores relevant facts, if he clings to a belief in the face of evidence against it, if he makes *ad hominem* arguments against other people.

But practicing objectivity is a challenge. Thinking takes effort. It involves the risk of error. And it can lead to disagreement with others. As Ayn Rand noted, these are among the factors that have made mysticism and dogmatism appealing to many people. Even among those committed to reason, however, those factors can operate on the margins to compromise objectivity. In addition, psychologists have identified cognitive biases we are vulnerable to, like confirmation bias—one of several we will consider later.

In the circumstances, I have found it helpful to use certain self-monitoring questions as a way to stay on track. I have extracted them from my experience as a teacher of logic and rationality, and from observations of my own efforts and those of others to practice objectivity. The questions are:

1. What is my purpose?
2. How do I know?
3. Am I sure?
4. Is that the real reason?
5. What would I take as evidence that I'm wrong?
6. Does anything matter more to me than the truth?
7. Can I be objective now?

I have formulated these as questions rather than a set of rules or a checklist because questions are more open-ended. They invite exploration and self-awareness—even when the answer is "Yes." They become habitual (hence my adaptation of Steven Covey's famous title, *The Seven Habits of Highly Effective People*). The questions themselves are things we need to ask consciously. What becomes habitual is the practice of raising the questions in the course of thinking.

So let's begin. The Highly Objective Person Asks....

1. What Is My Purpose?

Thinking is a goal-directed activity, a self-directed process. So the first question to ask is, "What is my goal?" The central aim is to acquire knowledge, to identify facts, through observation and reasoning. That's what the fields of epistemology and logic are mainly concerned with. But we can have many other ancillary goals.

- We may just want to understand something without (yet) forming a judgment about it, as in understanding what an author is saying, or what the argument for a government policy is. "OK, I get it" does not mean I agree. It means I understand the point.
- We may engage in speculation, letting our minds range over possible explanations, possible scenarios, possible plans of action. This is normally an important first step before we can begin looking for reasons and evidence to reach a conclusion or decide on a plan.
- We may engage in imagination. This is obviously important in artistic creativity, as when a novelist creates a narrative. But imagination plays a crucial role in all creativity, from an inventor imagining a new machine, to a businessman conceiving of a new marketing strategy, to a couple imagining life in a new city, and on and on.

All of those are perfectly reasonable things to do. But we need to know what we are doing. Mixing up goals leads to confusion and error. If I am trying to understand someone's behavior, for example, imagining a possible motive is not in itself evidence for the judgment that it actually *was* his motive.

Knowing my goal is also important in interacting with other people. What am I doing in this exchange with someone else?

- Am I just passing along information, like giving directions to a stranger in my town, or providing research to decision-makers on a project?
- Am I just having a conversation, catching up, sharing ideas and experiences, enjoying the pleasure of each other's company as an end in itself?
- Am I trying to persuade you? I'm talking politics with someone, or discussing strategy in a business meeting, or talking with my spouse about a family decision. I have a point of view; I want to give my reasons and convince the other person.
- Am I just trying to understand someone? I'm not trying to persuade, but it's not idle conversation, either; I have a specific cognitive goal of understanding his point of view, or a choice he made.

In exchanges with others, the possibility of mixing up goals is multiplied: It's important to be clear about the other person's goals as well as your own. You may simply be trying to understand me, for example, and ask a question just for information, but I may take it as an argument or criticism that I then answer with a counter-argument. Suppose I'm running a business and just had to lay off some of the staff.

> You: "That's too bad. Were you close to any of them?"
> I: "Some of them, yes. But look, it's a business, not a charity. I can't keep people on at a loss."

My answer is needlessly defensive because I didn't understand your goal.

Another example: I wronged you in some way, and I want to rectify the situation. Part of an apology is trying to make my action intelligible to you. You ask "Why did you do that?" and I try to explain what was going through my mind. But there's a difference between explaining and excusing. If you take what I say as an excuse—an attempt to get off the hook, morally speaking—then you have misunderstood my goal. And I could help avoid the misunderstanding by making it clear that I'm just explaining, not excusing.

2. How Do I Know?

When we perceive something, the awareness of reality is direct; you see the tree, hear the bell, taste the apple, and so forth. But conceptual knowledge—the things we can put into words—is processed, not direct. Starting from perception, it involves inference, interpretation, evidence. It's a self-directed process, building up to the vast store of knowledge we all have. Any new question we consider and try to answer relies on that enormous context of background knowledge. Conceptual thought is also fallible. There are many ways the process can go wrong—through evasion, jumping to conclusions, incomplete evidence, and other sources of error. That's why we need the concept of objectivity in the first place. We often need to step back and ask, How do I know that? How did I get to that conclusion? Why do I think it's true? Reality is not a book with all the answers in the back. Conclusions are only as good as the process that produced them, and we are responsible for conducting that process.

But here's the challenge: The reasons behind what we believe become automated once we have reached a conclusion. All of the prior knowledge that grounds our thoughts in reality is subconscious; we can hold only a limited amount of information in conscious attention. Yet objectivity requires that we re-activate relevant background knowledge in order to double-check results.

We obviously cannot do that for all of our knowledge at once. But there are questions I have found useful in calling up relevant information as needed:

What's my source?

Much of what we know depends on what we have learned from others—history books, teachers, scientific reports, the media, friends—and therefore depends on the reliability of the source. I think that Social Security should be privatized, and one reason (not the fundamental one) is that the rate of return on a private retirement account would be more than the implicit return from Social Security. Where did I get that? Oh, it was a study by the Cato Institute. Can I rely on it? Cato is good, but they have a libertarian agenda. Maybe I should look for a second source.

Do I remember it well?

Memory is a vital cognitive asset; thinking would be literally impossible without it. But it is fallible, both in ways we're all familiar with and in more subtle ways that psychologists have researched. Checking memory of facts is fairly easy, thanks to the internet. Memories of people, events, and experiences in our personal lives are harder to confirm. As a general rule, we remember best the things that got our full attention at the time, especially if we put them into words. So putting things in words at the time improves the accuracy of later memory.

But we should be wary of hindsight bias. That's the tendency to think, once we know the outcome of an event or decision, that we could have or should have predicted the outcome in advance. A dam breaks and floods a village below. Why didn't the engineers see that coming and shore up the dam? A relationship ended when a conflict of values and expectations with my partner came to the surface. I should have known that that was inevitable. Recriminations like these show that hindsight is not in fact 20/20. The outcome of an event, or the success or failure of a plan or relationship, is usually the result of many factors, only some of which we could have known in advance. Knowing the outcome reveals which factor was the operative cause, but it's often a mistake—and a source of unearned guilt—to assume that that knowledge was available beforehand.

What am I assuming?

All thinking takes place within a context, a framework that includes the issue at hand, the alternative possibilities, and the relevant evidence. Does my framework include any assumptions I should question? Ayn Rand was a genius at uncovering implicit philosophical assumptions, often by questioning seeming opposites. Like the dichotomy between selfish and selfless–sacrificing others to oneself or oneself to others: Rand explained why human life does not require sacrifices either way. We can apply this method on any issue, at any level. For example:

- You have been appointed head of a team in your company. Your second in command is Tom, who wanted that position, too. In meetings he asks many questions about your plans and decisions; you become irritated and answer brusquely. You take the questions as challenges, an effort to undermine you and get the role for himself. But is that assumption true? Is that the only explanation for Tom's questions? An alternative is that he's deeply committed to the project and just wants to make sure he understands your strategy.
- Natalie is talking with her therapist about her fear of conflict, which is preventing her from advancing at work. The therapist wants to help her find the assumptions that underlie the fear.

    - "Suppose a colleague was unfair to you. What would happen if you called him on it?"
    - "He would think I'm a hostile person."
    - "Is criticism necessarily hostile?"

The conversation could go in many directions from here. The point is that our fears, like other emotions, come from implicit premises we have embraced. Finding and challenging those assumptions is the key to dealing with many psychological problems.

3. Am I Sure?

If you claim to know something, you are claiming that it's certain. Certainty is a measure of the degree of evidence we have for an idea. A conclusion is certain if it is consistent with all the evidence, and if no rival conclusion is also consistent with the body of evidence. This is a more formal statement of the standard used in criminal law: proof beyond a reasonable doubt. If we have only partial evidence, or more than one conclusion is consistent with that evidence, then the most we can say is that a given conclusion is probable. An important element in the standard of certainty is that we must be alert to any evidence that there is more evidence to be obtained. Dr. Weiss in our opening example was confident in his diagnosis of depression, but he could not claim objective certainty: His diagnosis was not consistent with the patient's anomalous symptoms, and those symptoms implied there was more evidence to seek.

Certainty is the brass ring, the prize for thinking. But the prize is hard-won. It takes work to achieve certainty—real certainty, what we call epistemological certainty as an aspect of objective knowledge—as opposed to psychological certainty, the *feeling* of being sure. That feeling is extremely powerful. People crave certainty. They find it intolerable to have questions they can't answer, or deal with phenomena they can't explain, so they take shortcuts, leaping to conclusions, making up facts, elevating hunches into truths. They turn to "get certain quick" schemes like faith or authority, just as people who seek wealth without effort fall for get-rich-quick schemes.

Putting those irrational schemes aside, the rational pursuit of certainty still poses real challenges. To meet those challenges, fields like science and law have specific methodologies for assessing whether the evidence adds up to a proof of a conclusion. But there are guidelines we can use across the board.

Is certainty possible in this case?

There is much we can be certain about, from the direct awareness of our environment, to established scientific theories like the atomic theory of matter, to the axioms of logic and philosophy. You can count on the law of identity: A is A. But in the course of living our lives, we spend much of our time in the realm of probability. That's necessarily true in planning for the future. If I marry her, will I be happy ten years out? Will your business plan work? And it's true for complex situations past or present as well as future, like the causes of the financial crisis in 2008. There's abundant evidence about many causal factors, but their relative degrees of causal impact is not, and perhaps never will be, known with full certainty. A useful heuristic in this context is to assign a probability to your leading hypothesis. What are the chances that the marriage will last ten years, that the business will be profitable, etc.? The heuristic is useful because it creates an anchor point which we can adjust up or down as events unfold and we acquire more information.

Wanna bet?

Annie Duke is a world-class poker champ and business consultant. In *Thinking in Bets,* she explains the value of a related heuristic: asking how much you would be willing to bet that your belief is true. The heuristic is a version of the probability estimate just described, but it adds a money incentive.

> Being asked if we are willing to bet money on [a belief] makes it much more likely that we will examine our information in a less biased way, be more honest with ourselves about how sure we are of our beliefs, and be more open to updating and calibrating our beliefs. (66)

This heuristic obviously applies to the realm of probability. But it also applies to issues in ethics, politics, and philosophy. As an Objectivist philosopher, I believe that we can achieve genuine certainty in this realm. But certainty is contextual. It means that a conclusion is the only alternative consistent with all the evidence *within the available context of one's knowledge*. For an active mind, that context is continually expanding. "Wanna bet?" is a useful question to point us toward ways to deepen and expand that context.

For example, an implication of the Objectivist political philosophy is that nationalized health care (single-payer, "Medicare for all") is unjust. "Wanna bet?" Well, why do I believe that? What's the basis in the principles of individual rights and the function of government? If someone challenges my view, can I explain those premises clearly? Is health care unique as a service, not well served by voluntary trade in a free market? Why or why not? Thinking of my position as a bet points me toward those questions, as things I may need to understand more fully. And it gets me to rank my degree of confidence in this view against other things I'm sure of.*

Betting on the truth of a belief does not imply uncertainty. It is not based on the skeptical view that we can never be certain, that probability is the best we can do. After all, we estimate probabilities on the basis of facts we already know. Perhaps you estimate that your new business has a 60% chance of success. Success is probable only, but you based your estimate on facts: demand for your product, the threat of competition, the funds you

---

* Strictly speaking, the probability of an outcome like a coin toss is not the same as probability as a degree of evidence, an epistemological state. The probability of an event or outcome is a fact of reality: heads or tails, 50/50; probability of rain today, 60%. Probability as a degree of evidence is a fact about us, about the state of our knowledge. In light of the difference, it may be safer to use a different scale to assess our degree of confidence. E.g., on a scale of 1 to 10, how sure am I?

have to invest, the historical rate of success and failure for similar start-ups, etc. For most if not all of these factors, you can know them with certainty. Indeed, if you have done a good job acquiring all this information, you can be (epistemologically) certain *that* your business has a 60% chance of success in reality.

Thinking in bets, in other words, has a positive function. It is a heuristic to motivate self-awareness about the reasons for a belief or decision, and to foster alertness to further evidence.

4. What Would I Take As Evidence That I'm Wrong?

This is a hard question to ask ourselves and answer honestly. But it's an important question because we are often working uphill against confirmation bias—the tendency to look for and take account of evidence supporting a conclusion while ignoring, downplaying, or failing to seek evidence against it. In our opening example, Tyler is engaging in confirmation bias. He is not open to the case for raising the minimum wage. He is not listening to the case his opponent is making; he searches only for evidence to support his own view. He may be right in what he believes, but he is not entitled to be certain because he has closed his mind to any counter-evidence.

Confirmation bias takes many forms.

- When we are angry at someone, our minds tend to multiply examples of how that person has wronged or offended us and to forget the other times when the person was fair or kind.
- Once we notice what might be a pattern in the events and people around us, we easily generalize, and then pay more attention to positive examples than to counter-evidence. I suspect the economy is slowing down, so my attention is drawn to things that confirm the trend: I start noticing every house with a "For Sale" sign, every drop in the stock market, etc.
- We tend to rely on media sources that share our views rather than seeking news and ideas that challenge them.

The best counter to confirmation bias is to ask what you would take as evidence against what you believe. And the best way to do that is to start with another question: What is the alternative to my belief? What is the rival position on this issue? Then you can consider what evidence someone holding that position would cite, what arguments he would offer if you were debating the issue. On the issue of national health care, for example, what reasons do advocates have? Put aside your view for a moment and try to get inside the head of an advocate. How does the world look to him? What leads him to think socialized health care is good?

It's rare, in my experience, that this exercise actually changes my mind. Nevertheless it has tremendous value. If I am discussing the issue with such an advocate, I need to start by understanding his position; otherwise the exchange is useless. But the real benefit is that I gain a deeper understanding of the issue and of my own reasons for what I believe. Psychological research has found that merely asking people to consider how they might be wrong, and to generate alternative positions or hypotheses, is an effective way to avoid confirmation bias.

Have you ever heard someone say about people who disagree with him, especially in politics, "Why don't they get it? Can't they just see?" Have you felt that impatience yourself? It's a warning sign of bias. None of our knowledge, except for axioms like A is A, is literally self-evident. But convictions often feel that way because we have automated all the thinking and prior knowledge that led us to that conviction. Discussing one's viewpoint with people of different viewpoints, or at least trying to imagine what an opponent might say, is an excellent way to bring the reasons for your own belief back into conscious awareness.

Of course there are exceptions. People who claim that truth is a subjective construction are not worth dealing with (unless you are a philosopher, in which case it's an unwelcome professional necessity). It's hopeless to argue with conspiracy theorists, or Flat Earthers. Life is short, irrationality is endless. Spending time and energy engaging with someone who has displayed consistent irrationality is the loss of time that could be spent engaging with more reasonable and honest partners.

5. Is That the Real Reason?

When I was in high school, starting to date, I had my share of disappointments. Sometimes, when I worked up my nerve to ask a girl out, I'd get a nice decline. "Oh, thank you, that's sweet. But I promised my sister I'd be at her graduation. Maybe another time." Maybe another time—that's a straw to grasp at. So I'd try again. "Thanks, that sounds nice. But I have to study for the math test." OK, now what? Try again? My buddies and I had a rule of thumb. If she turns you down three times, you're out. No matter how kind or plausible her excuses, the real reason is that she's just not interested.

Declining an invitation or request with a non-essential reason, in order to spare the other person's feelings, is not confined to teen-agers. It's a commonplace of adult life. When your real reason for declining is that you are not interested in the invitation, or unwilling to meet the request, the other reasons you give may be true, but there's still a kind of lie by omission, white though it may be.

The question, "Is that my real reason?" cuts deeper, though. We have multiple reasons for virtually any belief or decision. But those reasons are not all on a par. Some are more essential than others. Some are better grounded than others. To be objective, we should be aware of these differences. Tyler, in our opening example, is a case in point: His debating points against raising the minimum wage are not his real reason, which is his belief in economic freedom and the right of people to contract on any terms they accept.

Another case in point: I'm defending capitalism to someone who is inclined to socialism. At some point he asks who would own the roads. How could private companies in a competitive market own and manage city streets? I launch into an explanation of libertarian solutions.... But then I stop and ask myself, is this the real issue? Does my belief in capitalism—or my opponent's belief in socialism—hang on the issue of roads? If I conceded that government has to provide the roads, would he then embrace the rest of my free-market view? Of course not. Neither of us is presenting the real reasons for our pro-capitalist and pro-socialist views, the reasons that really underlie our convictions.

Overreactions are another occasion to ask our question. A salesman comes back to the office after a series of client visits that produced no sales. Intensely frustrated, he gets furious at an assistant over a typo in a product brochure. Yes, the typo is a mistake; it may deserve a mild rebuke. But the salesman's anger is an overreaction. The real reason he's angry is that the trip was not successful. In the name of objectivity, he owes it to himself (and to his assistant) to recognize that fact.

And then there is rationalization, the most serious and non-objective way of evading the real reasons for an action. Rationalization is a defense mechanism using the tools of reason to evade a threatening belief by persuading oneself of a less threatening one. The "sour grapes" phenomenon is a minor instance: She turned me down for a date. Well, I really wasn't that interested—despite the fact that I really was. More significant cases involve attempts to explain away actions that violate our standards by inventing justifications. I'm managing a team at work, my boss asks for an update, and I exaggerate our progress. What I told my boss is a lie, but it's easy to invent excuses. I was under a lot of pressure, or my exaggeration didn't interfere with the project, or I was trying to protect the team. Such excuses are endless, but they all have a goal: of disguising the real reason for my lie, which was to avoid acknowledging my lack of progress and having to face the boss's disapproval.

6. Does Anything Matter More to Me than the Truth?

Objectivity includes a commitment to reality, to finding the truth; and a commitment to use reason as the means. We have seen some of the ways we can misuse reason in ways that create obstacles to finding the truth. But if we are not committed to finding the truth in the first place, then rational thought has lost its purpose altogether. Rationality, as Ayn Rand put it, means "that one must never place any value or consideration whatsoever above one's perception of reality." In that respect, the most important question to ask ourselves is whether anything is more important than the truth.

Many things can supersede truth as a goal, too many to list. But here are a few.

Threatening facts

Fear is often the motive for evading facts that threaten some value. A parent scolds a child harshly out of sheer frustration but doesn't want to think about it later because it threatens his self-image as a good parent. His view of himself is more important than the truth. Carla, in our earlier example, makes up a story to explain her husband's behavior; she values feeling secure in her marriage more than the truth. A professor has a strong belief in 2nd Amendment rights but is afraid of conflict, so he keeps his view to himself even in discussions about guns and crime. Avoiding conflict is more important than stating the truth.

Fear of error

Thinking is fallible. In addition to culpable errors like evasion or wishful thinking, there are innocent errors we can make from incomplete information, mistakes in reasoning, and other factors. Fear of error, ironically, can take precedence over the commitment to truth. On the one hand, people can become rigid in their views, unwilling to think about counter-evidence or even considerations that might call for some revision. Their views may well be based on solid reasoning, rather than blind dogma, but the views are now fixed and closed. They identify with their views in a way that would make openness to revision a threat to their sense of self. On the other hand, there is epistemological timidity. For some people, the fear of error leads them to be tentative about claiming certainty, even when it is justified. Who knows when some new fact will come along to disprove my conclusion? We can see this syndrome in people who hate to make decisions, always stalling by asking for more information.

But we can and should take error as an opportunity, not a threat. When I began teaching logic in college, I would sometimes make a mistake in working out a problem on the blackboard. I was embarrassed to screw up in front of my students. But then I realized it provided a "teachable moment." Seeing the instructor get it wrong eased the students' anxiety about making mistakes themselves. Talking about why I erred gave them more insight about the methods I was teaching them. And it showed them—and me—that acknowledging the fact is more important than my professional pride. Finding an error in one's view is unsettling, but it is an important signal of something wrong in our grasp of reality, as pain is a signal of something wrong in our physical bodies. Instead of fearing error, we can take it as an opportunity to expand our grasp of facts.

What matters more, being right or getting it right?

Most of us spend time in meetings at work, or with spouses, or in other groups. There are issues on the table that require a decision, a consensus position, or an outcome of some other sort. What is your goal in these cases? You have a plan, an opinion, or a point of view. What matters most—that you persuade people to adopt your plan, or adopt your view as the consensus? Or is it to find the best plan, the best-supported position, whether it's yours, someone else's, or the unexpected product of discussion? In a political argument, what matters most—winning the argument, or learning from it? Most of us have been in situations with people who treat argument as a blood sport; they're out to win and crush the opposing side. Some of us have been that person at times.

So the question to ask is: What matters more, *being* right or *getting it right*? Tyler, our libertarian, is an example of someone who needs to be right; that's the source of his aggressive argumentative attack against his opponent. This approach is not objective. Winning the argument is more important to him than identifying facts—even if he's right about the minimum wage. And his approach reflects a lack of independence. People who are independent thinkers don't depend on the agreement of others. Persuading others may be a practical need in some cases. But for an independent person, agreement is never a more important concern than truth. Richard Whately, a 19th century English poet and clergyman, put the point well: "It is one thing to wish to have truth on our side, and another to wish sincerely to be on the side of truth."

Objectivity and self-esteem

The fundamental point of this section, and of this work as a whole, is to recognize that reality is our friend, not an enemy, not a threat, not a harsh mistress to our thoughts. It's the foundation of all our thoughts and the standard for guiding them. Yes, it sometimes offers tough love—unwelcome facts, threatening facts, facts that challenge our beliefs, facts that require painful decisions. But it's foolish to base one's self-esteem on confirmation of what we believe or feel, which may be in conflict with the facts. We can base our self-esteem instead on the ability of our conscious minds to grasp and accept facts as they are.

This attitude is sometimes described as intellectual humility, which has become a buzzword in business as well as academia. The description is dead wrong. Humility is seen as the antidote to arrogance, overconfidence in one's judgment, defensiveness about admitting mistakes, etc. Those traits are indeed nonobjective. But humility is not objective, either. Dictionaries define the term as meaning deference, meekness, awareness of one's failings, and a sense of inferiority. Those traits are the polar opposite of the fundamental trait of a truly objective person: pride in having the strength of mind to grasp reality as it is.

7. Can I Be Objective Now?

Our final question is a kind of failsafe device. Objectivity is a universal virtue; it applies across all the topics we think about, and all the cognitive purposes we pursue, during every waking hour. But there are obstacles that can make it hard to think objectively, and sometimes the best solution is to call it a day.

Is the light switch on?

Thinking is a capacity with a biological basis. It takes effort. It consumes energy—some 20% of the body's total budget goes to supporting brain activity. Thinking is also one function among many others, including emotions, sense-perception, and internal functions like regulating hormones. Thinking is a voluntary function; we can normally choose where to direct our attention and whether to raise or lower our level of focus. The light switch is under our control. But that choice operates within biological constraints. Fatigue is one example, the distinctively mental fatigue that makes it hard to focus. Distraction is another, when too many thoughts, issues, tasks, and feelings are clamoring for attention. Have you ever found yourself at your desk, with piles of papers, scattered To-Do lists, a billowing inbox, and no idea where to start? I certainly have. If fatigue, distraction, or anything else limits our ability to think clearly and objectively, it's time to take a break.

Can I deal with this now?

Intense emotions of fear, anger, sorrow, and frustration can overwhelm the ability to think objectively. Instead of simply having the emotion, you experience the emotion as *having you*. Marriage counselors have observed that couples in conflict can become gridlocked; they try to talk the problem through, but the issues become inflated, positions grow more polarized; one or both feels as if their very identity is at stake. The usual advice is that more talk will not help. It has become part of the problem, not a solution, at least for now, until they can bring a higher level of objectivity to their issues. In situations like these, the rational thing to do may be to call time-out. That strategy is not just for 3-year-olds.

Conclusion

As I said at the beginning, objectivity is both a virtue and a skill. And in both respects our ability to think objectively increases with use. Highly objective people use questions like the ones we have discussed to guide the conscious process of thinking, and over time the questions become automated: it becomes easier and more habitual to raise them. In many of the examples I have used, the issues are of minor importance in themselves, but the choice to be objective is important nonetheless, in building the habit of aligning oneself with reality. Conversely, small actions of evasion and wishful thinking may not have serious consequences at the time, but they build a habit of fleeing from unwelcome facts. Dr. Weiss's patient, for example, may not be harmed by the antidepressant, but if Weiss ignores anomalous symptoms in a case of heart disease or cancer, the effect may be fatal. Carla may get short-term relief by inventing a story about her husband, but when the truth comes out, the marriage dissolves, and she is faced with life on her own, she will function with a diminished ability to think and choose wisely. Virtues are acquired by practice. So are vices.

Above all I urge you not to think of objectivity as a duty, a cold necessity, or a grudging acceptance of facts. There is peace and serenity is being aligned with reality. There's excitement in learning new things by checking our premises and using error as a step toward discovery. There's more chance for intimate and productive relationships when we are honest and open with each other.

In the name of your best life, objectivity is worth the effort.

Printed in Japan
落丁、乱丁本のお問い合わせは
Amazon.co.jp カスタマーサービスへ

5996639R00019